CAVORTING WITH TIME/ MALINS

Cavorting with Time
Recent Work Press + Ampersand Duck
Canberra, Australia

ISBN: 978-0-6482579-1-2

Copyright © Jacqui Malins 2018
facebook.com/jacqui.malins.art/

All rights reserved. This book is copyright. Except for private study, research, criticism or reviews as permitted under the Copyright Act, no part of this book may be reproduced stored in a retrieval system, or transmitted in any form by any means without prior written permission. Enquiries should be addressed to the publisher.

Design & layout: Caren Florance
carenflorance.com

Cover image and illustrations: Jacqui Malins

recentworkpress.com

CAVORTING WITH TIME
A working script

by
Jacqui Malins

Recent Work Press
Ampersand Duck
2018

CAVORTING WITH TIME: COMPLETE

Foreword vii
Key 1

1. Bow to your partner 3
2. Mystique 5
3. Indigestion 7
4. Reconnaissance 8
5. Flesh 12
6. Atlas 14
7. In your own time 17
8. Time – my tattooist . . . 19
9. Inheritance 22
10. Infinite skin 24
11. Clouds 28
12. Unconformity 30
13. Thaw 34
14. Six thoughts 35
15. Diving 37
16. Washing your bones 38
17. War cry 42
18. A turn with death 46
19. Time 49

Notes 51
Biography & thanks 52

FOREWORD

Most of the poems in 'Cavorting with time' were written in the first half of 2017. 'Time, my tattooist' was the first, written in 2016. It started me on a process of research and reading to find new frames and lenses for viewing ageing and mortality. Philosophy and feminism were rich resources, as I was confronted by my internalised ageism in the face of my middle years.

'Cavorting with Time' is presented as a working performance script. At the time of publication of this first edition, I have performed selections of the work in different combinations. They are outlined in the acknowledgements on Page 45.

During late 2017 and early 2018, musician Julia Horvath and I developed a 'Cavorting with time' performance for spoken word and cello. This first edition includes annotation of the poems which have been set with (overwhelmingly, original) music by Julia. The key to these annotations is on the next page.

Future editions of this working script will be updated with notes and annotation of subsequent arrangements for performance.

CAVORTING WITH TIME/ MALINS

KEY

𝄢 = Cello start

𝄥 = Cello finish

⌒ = Cello bowed

" " " = Cello plucked (*pizzicato*)

1. BOW TO YOUR PARTNER

How will you dance with time?

  Jig?

        Gavotte?

                March?

                        Romp?

I've carried my dignity so long,
like a pile of books upon my head.
Top-heavy with enormous dignity,
to bend would skew my gravity.
So I stood, rigid.

Now I let this posture slide,
   cast poise aside

and kick up my heels to cavort with
my lifelong companion,

                Time.

2. MYSTIQUE

" " "

Some say the element of surprise
is essential for a love affair to last.

                        BOO!

Time shows me another view,   @

one more of her dimensions.
My crude human senses
perceive just a few.

She offered her fingertip to my spindly hand
at birth, to grip was instinctive.
To unfocused eyes she seemed
a vague and gentle presence.

She got stricter when I went to school,
ran away from me in the mornings
with the buses I missed and the popular kids.
But during playground days of tease
    and torment,
or boring Sunday afternoons,
a contrarian, she
                would
                hardly
                stir
                at
                all.

She never moves that slowly any more.

She is constant.
A metronome t i c k i n g ,
implacable pulse . . . . .
almost below the limit of hearing.
I can't keep a steady pace
so she seems to drag or race.

If I look her in the eyes
in the mirror, unblinking,
see her marks and signs
without flinching
instead of dragging, laggard, unwilling,
I might learn to strut and shimmy.

To dance the life away.

¢

3. INDIGESTION

Fear of you has been served to me
both hot and cold.
I learned your taste to be
ugliness, decrepitude.
Overcooked and bitter,
you trigger heartburn.
In dyspeptic misanthropy
I deny you.
Asked my age, I close my ears.
Told I don't show my years,
I glow, self satisfied.

Still,
you are here.

4. RECONNAISSANCE

☊

At seventy my father says
he feels the same person
he was at forty-five.

☋

Am I the same person I was that long ago?

Time, wind the handle of your infernal,
    eternal machine.
and guide me on an impossible journey
    to see.
Only you can hold my hand
both now, and then.

Shoot me back across a space
laced with memory to face
myself at twenty.
I look into my eyes.
I recognise this woman from photographs, or
perhaps a book I read?

I am not
the same mind.

I am not all that hair.
I am not that face, that discontented glare.

                    She is in me.
                    I outgrew her.

I will not squeeze into her narrow frame
                                  again.

Time, turn your crank the other way,
                              reel me in
to catch my breath for an instant
in the present.

Now cast me out across a space
traced with imagination, both brighter
and more precarious than memory.
The lense of now distorts my view,
the present bends the future.

At twenty I didn't grasp the task.
Now I think I sense how vast the gulf
From here to seventy, though
it looms up fast.

Let's start with what I know.
Mash my face with my mother's,
    my father's,
        the great grandmother's,
            whose cheekbones show
                through my skin.

Is this my seventy-year-old simulacrum?
She looks smaller than me, but I sense
she is bigger inside than I can see.

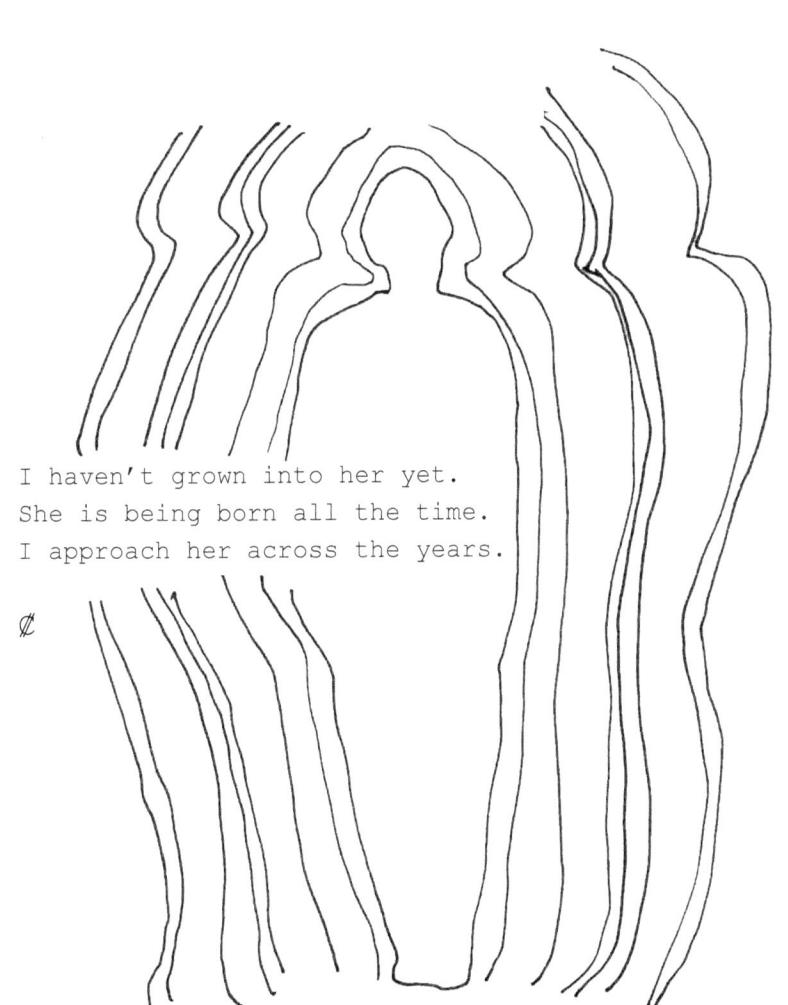

```
I haven't grown into her yet.
She is being born all the time.
I approach her across the years.

¢
```

5. FLESH

Chop a few bits off
and I will still be me –
                                to some degree.

You can't sift me out of myself
                   like wheatgerm from flour,
shuck my mind like an oyster from its shell,
peel my spirit from its cells.

The cartesian cutthroat flays me.

I am no ghost driving a meat machine,
and who wants to transcend the
texture of grass under feet or the
smell of the air or the taste of a kiss?

Even cramps and aches are signs of life
and my body is in the grip of Time.
'You are only as young as you feel' and
'age is a state of mind' won't release me.

I can choose how much I pay attention
to my reflection in your eyes
and whether I buy your judgement,
but I can't escape Time's ministrations.

⊙

I will cultivate my Stockholm syndrome,
work diligently at this arranged marriage,
tend to the intimacy between Time and me.
My fusion will be completed by her alchemy.
No pure spirit will be distilled from

        my flesh,

                burned off at death

                        into heaven.

∅

6. ATLAS

Time is my cartographer, my raw hide her
She stretches my vellum to fit the world
Records my fall at three with a stitched
tropical infection at forty with an
Her topographic document includes
the glyphs of acne, fresh and past
freckles of anglo settlement under
chewed fingertip peninsulas,
stretch-marked contours,
tributaries of the failure to use
the straight-line blades of kitchen

A fortune-telling friend saw my future
in an extract of this atlas
as small as my palm.
My lover reads the whole volume.
Still the future is a mystery
only Time will tell.

blank.
she maps.
half-moon,
embossed seal.

austral sun,

washing up gloves or sunscreen,
scars.

7. IN YOUR OWN TIME

I thought that in my grandmother's day
you got to a certain age
stripped off your sex and
stepped into the costume that waited –
wrinkled mask, permed wig, elastic waist,
sensible shoes.
Shuffled off, stoop-shouldered,
    in a cloud of talcum powder.

Now I look toward a gauntlet
of brandishing hands and clamouring voices
proffering choices – 'don't grow old,
   stay young,
       grow old disgracefully, be tasteful,
   let yourself go, stay fit,
be natural, use all the help you can get'.

Don't become a caricature.
Don't become your mother.
Don't become a caricature of your mother.

Try but don't try too hard.

Simone de Beauvoir said that age
is a costume in which we appear,
but we ourselves cannot see.
If we are in the dark, let's dress ourselves
by feel, not fear.

8. TIME - MY TATTOOIST

I wear fake tattoos of feathers.
I've thought about permanent ink,
   but what design?
I remember the pastel Monet print that once
adorned my room
                and I don't trust my taste
to stand the test of time.

But Time tests us all - she can be
         my tattooist, she can choose.
She has already punctuated my knuckles
   with stronger lines,
traced stacked bracelets at my wrists,
etched horizons across my forehead,
fanned crows-feet like the shadow of
                                false lashes.

She started subtle.
Knew I wasn't up for anything too bold. Yet.
But as, each year, I fear less,
she dares me, eggs me on.

She is starting on a pair
            of delicate spiderweb gloves,
sketching a fine mesh across my décolleté,
designing a high lace collar that will go
   all   the way   up my neck

[19]

to my chin. At our next big session
she will start inking it in, making it
            indelible.
She thinks I should go all-out,
      with a full face cross-hatched mask.

'Go on', she taunts. 'Do it. Do it!'

One morning my mirror will tell me
                  that the night before
I stumbled, drunk, into her parlour and said
       'yes', which
            I, for sure, won't remember.

If her lines are like score marks on glass,
if you tap me sharply then
I will cleave,   shatter,   fall apart.

But they might be like fine wires that bind
me to myself.

A net to hold me together
in the face of inevitable dissolution.

¢

9. INHERITANCE
"""
Ⓠ

Your ancestry, you carry
with its skin and teeth and nose,
its money and privilege,
its poverty and oppression,
its something in between.
Your birthright and your birth wrong.
Your pragmatism and neuroses and values,
your unique combination of
springboard and lubricant,
mud and chains.

You have dragged this baggage
through your leg of the journey.
Unpacked and repacked,
dented and renovated.
Bought shiny new things,
received gifts, wanted and unwanted.
Picked bits and pieces up from the pavement.

Some you ate and turned to shit.
Some you polished with tongue and spit.
Some you can't change, some you will.
Some you regret not changing sooner.
Some came with indestructible manacles,
you can never throw it away.

With luck,
you will arrive
at the threshold of a house
that you must build

with this body,
this mind
and these possessions
to live in until
the end
of your days.

∅

10. INFINITE SKIN

Mandelbrot, father of fractals, wrote
'how long is the coast?'
Use a yardstick for one answer.
Your thumb for another –
The perimeter is longer when you take in
every wrinkle and cleft.
How long is my edge?
In age, my skin complicates
in fractal folds.
Measure it crudely if you want me small.
The finer your calibration,
the more you will see.
It once sprang in neat, plump arcs
that you could measure with compass
    and protractor,
define in relation to pi.
Now with the erosions of Time
    and the weather
I am corrugated, crenelated.
My body's conversation with space
elaborates.

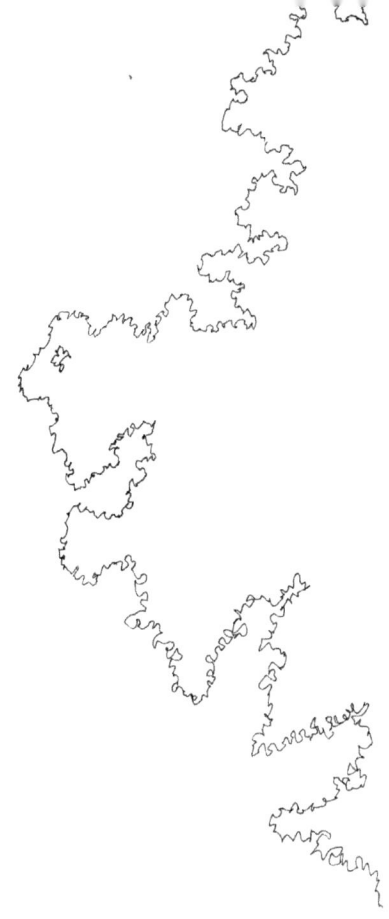

The self of yesterday, the day before
and all my days before that
fit comfortably inside.
I am all my selves at once.
As my skin thins I see
that this permeable membrane
is scarcely a border at all.

my name is - ? my name is
My name is... M y
My name is my
is my name is

name is my n
is My name is m.
is my name is

My name i

y name is   my name is
e is   my name is
me is   my name
name is my
e is   my name
ome is   my name
name

my name

11. CLOUDS
" " "

ⓠ

If the first signs
    of my surrender to Time
        are evinced by my mind
           should I resist?

I persist in seeing it
as the overseer who holds the whip,
keeping me in line,   awake,   alive.

But my mind doesn't carry the weight
Of mastery and memory alone.
The body also remembers -
a parent's embrace,
how to enfold a lover's shape,
the taste of crisp chips or flat lemonade,
how to press the keys,
flick the wrist,
hone the blade.

Ask some questions and
the body replies
before,   despite,   the mind.

I can hang on white-knuckled,
panic at each glitch and blip in cognition.
If I loosen my grip,
risk the sickening slip,
I might not fall,
but drift with the clouds,
dissolve into mist.

∅

12. UNCONFORMITY

An unconformity lies under Capital Hill.
A faultline where rocks made ages apart
were wrenched together.
They lie cheek by cheek,
Once moving, now still.

I am unconformity.

    My inside and out
                          are ages apart.

What do you see in the geological record
   of my face?
The crevasses into which beauty falls,

   screaming.

Cracks in the mirror, memento mori.
Schadenfreude that you are not as near
   to death as me.
Vexed scribblings of a child who
realises
       the party must end eventually.

I am unconformity.

This translucent skin should let the light
out lantern-like
but when I project my personality,
                        rare few can see.

You always read my woman's appearance
as the sum of me. You still do.
I have tried to see
the great withered baby I must be
for you to treat me with such exaggerated
patience, affected bonhomie.

I am unconformity.

The friction between inside and out chafes.
In infancy I didn't know
where I stopped and others began.
I hadn't learned shame for my flesh
                            and its functions.

My body had never been my own, nor my mind –
I had not known the luxury of privacy,
chosen what to share and what to keep.
I can't unknow a lifetime of autonomy.

The second time, dependency
is learning how to walk again
with a toddler's balance and awkward gait.
How to dance, like Ginger, not Fred,
      backwards, in high heels
                                with blisters.

13. THAW

Autumn and winter of our days, they say.
Our bodies stiffen, bones protrude
through worn skin like bare-limbed trees.
We watch one another freeze.
Dinner at six before the TV.

Or a chilly spring? Thawing
of the ice cube tray compartment shapes,
of all the roles we played?
The time to be solid, stand up unsupported,
hold myself together, is done.
Slump. Run down gullies,
puddle in the lowest contour.

Be a still mirror, reflect the world
    back to itself.
Be chopped and glinting in the breeze.

Dance with the light.
Keep changing.

14. SIX THOUGHTS

Chaperone or captor?
Time might trap me
in a bound and gagged body.
Her dark side.

Rustle this reliable steed
    out from under me.
Swap it for a recalcitrant animal.
That is me too.

Will it be easier
to accept the bodily ministrations
of those who love me
or those who don't?

Mortal life is not mortal combat.
No flurry of furious punches or kicks
will release Time's grip.

The face cream and hair dye
may disguise you from yourself
but Time knows who you are.

No armour or camouflage will enable you
to wriggle fishlike from her grasp,
vanish in a glamour of silver scales.

15. DIVING

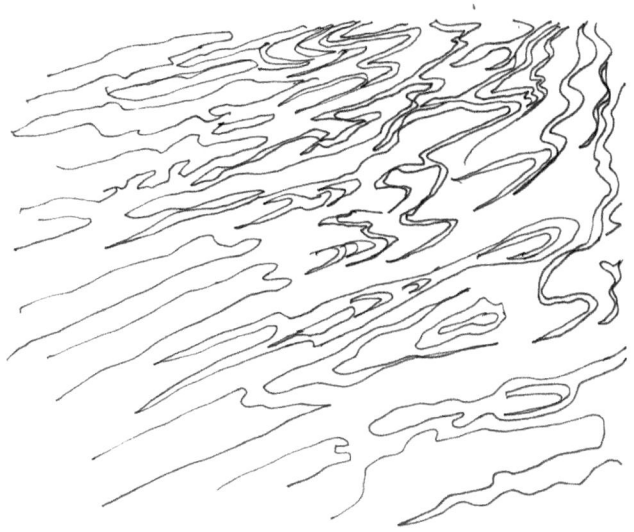

Swim lithe and wily through the currents,
then hover still in the shadow of a leaf.
Don't rage against the dying of the light,
follow it as long as your sight allows.
Then close your eyes and journey in.
Once an astronaut, now you are a deep-sea
diver.

16. WASHING YOUR BONES

If you still had ears to hear,
the scratch of this bristle brush
would set your bared teeth on edge,
send a shiver down your naked spine.
This pale scaffold held your life erect.
Soap slicks knobs and sockets burnished
by a generation of folding and unfolding.
Dirt and decay scour away, reveal
annealed fractures, and crevices
    you never saw,
not even with a hand mirror.
This contact is as intimate
    as your hip replacement, as
abrasive as arthritis. Bone grates bone
resonates through your domed skull
the same way you heard your own voice.

If you still had tongue to speak
you might tell me of the other side -
what life looks like from there.
You scrubbed up well!
Do you miss this bowling ball, these
    pick-up sticks?
I will relish my flesh while it lives
    and kicks,
hear the cries of the world with my ears
taste its tears with my tongue
feel the wind on my skin 'til it withers.
And for this night's festivities
I will lend you my muscles and ligaments,
link our fingers, press your hipbones
    to mine
and dance with you, cheek to jaw
the way we did before.

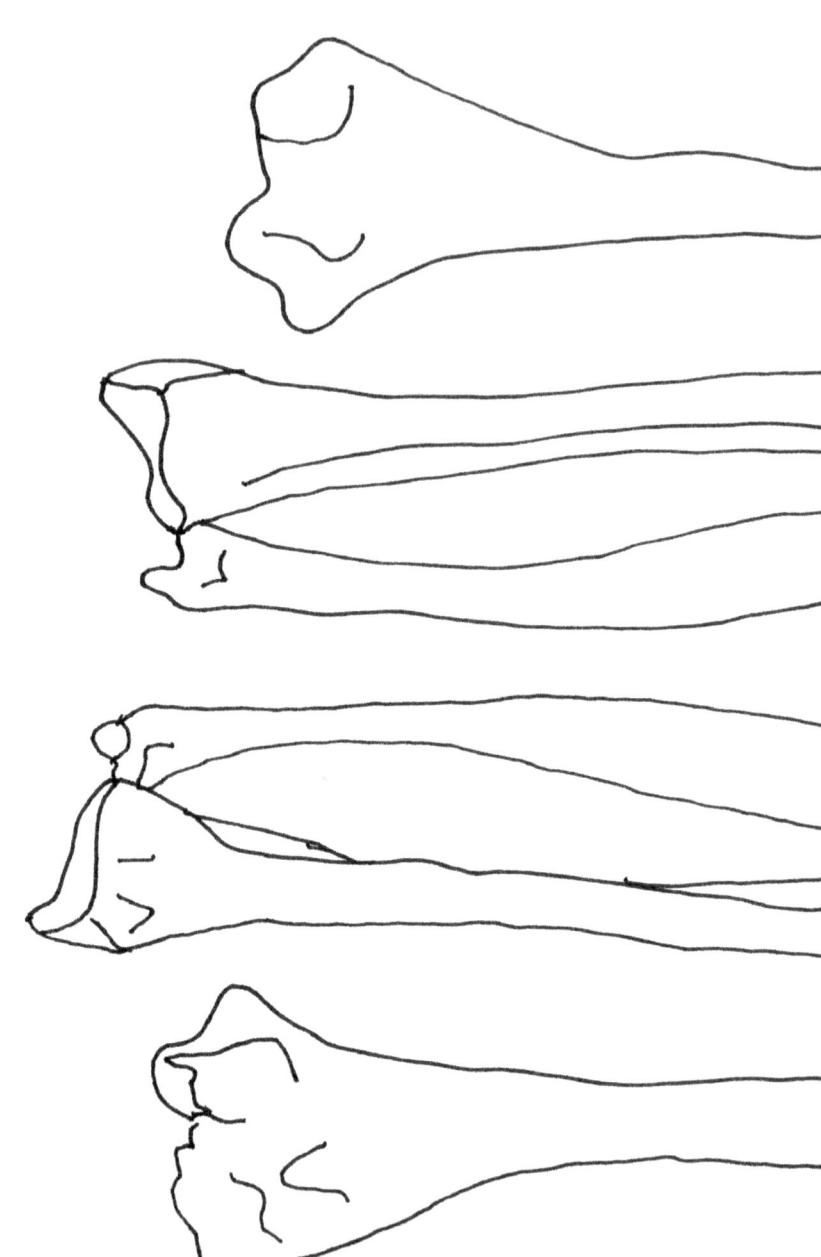

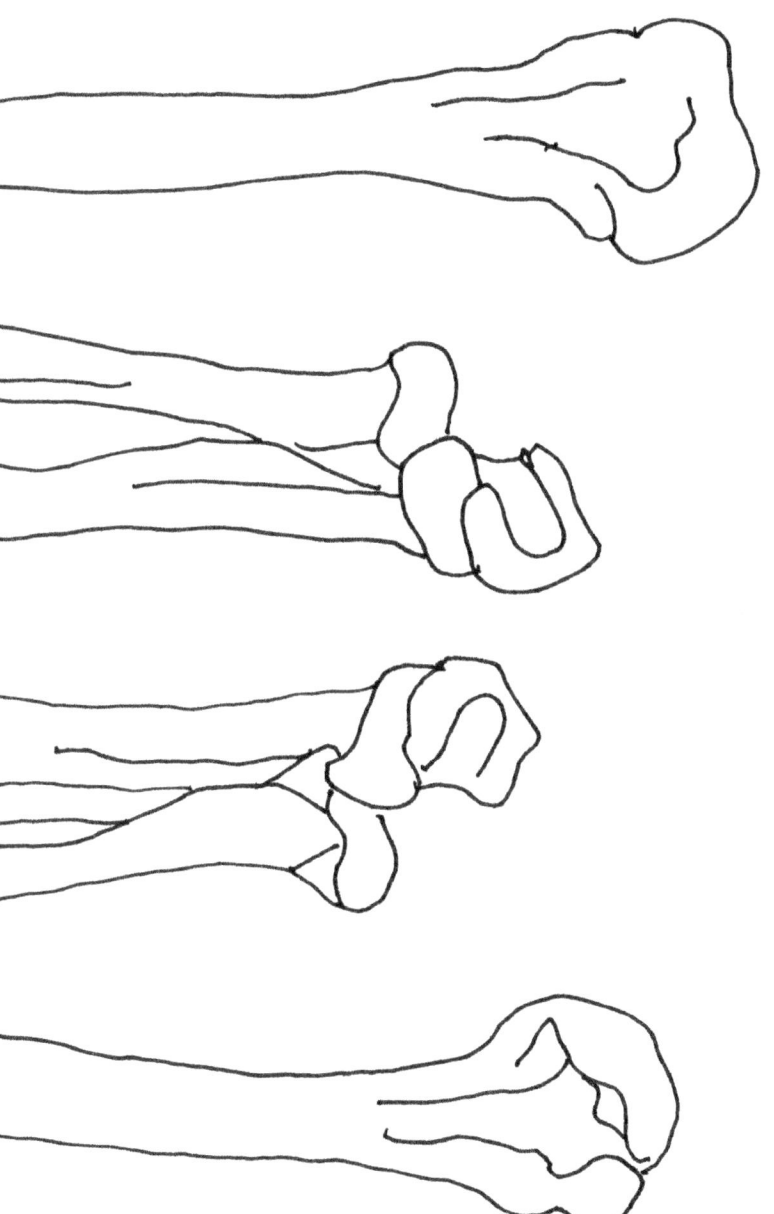

17. WAR CRY
༄

What are little old ladies made of?
☪
∅

What are little old ladies made of?
☪

Powder and pearls and frosted curls -
that's what little old ladies are made of.
∅

Old women - what are we made of?

☪
Young eyes can't pierce our camouflage,
their gaze slides away.
We remind them of things
they would rather forget,
have knowledge of things
they fear and regret.

Mothers and grandmothers.
Time, our sister.
Death, who walks with her,
They carry our life sentences
in their hands,
and rob our enemies of vengeance.

∅

Let's change everything when no one is
watching –
            which is always.

Our bodies do less

but our flesh knows more.
Let's use our powers of invisibility
for surveillance,
stealth missions,
covert operations.

When we are ready, with triumphant cries,
we will cast off our disguise,
and reveal ourselves,
the hags and crones of nightmare!

Gorgons, we will
roll our rheumy eyes,
flaunt our wrinkled skin
dangle empty sagging breasts
and swollen bosoms that smother men.
Our crumpled faces will
amplify our expressions to
deafening volume,
the tendons in our necks will
strain with the strength of our fibre,
our loose flesh will
undulate like earthquakes.
Then,

         with the bones of our enemies
and our foremothers
in our sparse white hair,

let's run together
[*loud*]   screaming
to throw our remaining days
                        on to the fire
                        of the future.

∉

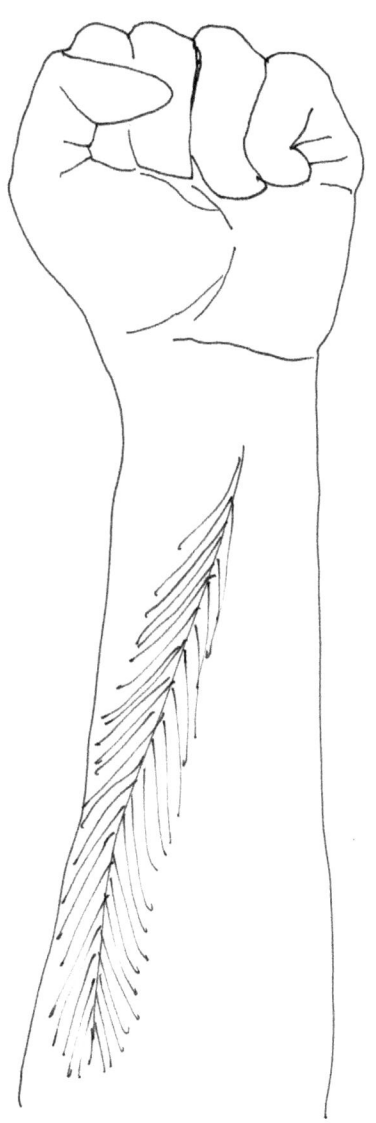

18. A TURN WITH DEATH

This waltz is progressive.
Some advance quickly.
Time is the mistress.

Death dances nearby.
The hungrier sister.
Time swings me near her, I shiver.

Time knows the steps.
She will pass me to Death when they're ready
for our turn about the floor.

Will my moment be quick?
A twirl and a dip? Or a grinding slow dance
Before Death's cool kiss?

Mere matter, I will slip through
her embrace,
to be caught
in the cupped hands
of Time.

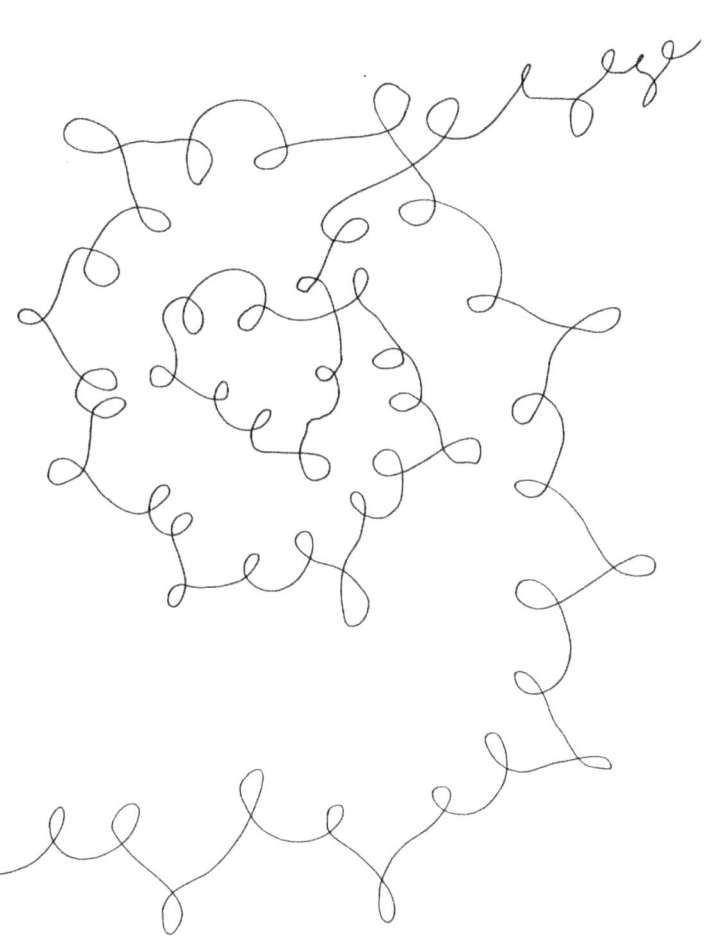

19. TIME

```
My guide and my goad,
                I can't live without you.
I don't want to.
Mark my skin, hair and bones.
Govern my body as it grows,
slows,
one day goes.
Having come to this ball,
     I will learn new steps
            to dance with you
                    for as long
                            as I am.
```

NOTES

'Time, my tattooist' (8) – first performed at the Canberra Slamboree at The Front Café and Gallery on 30 September 2016 (Canberra).

'Inheritance' (9) – first performed as part of a set supporting C J Bowerbird's 'The downfall of the main character' on 11 June 2017, Smith's Alternative (Canberra).

'Infinite skin' (10) - first performed as part of the 'Reverse Archaeology' concert with the Griffyn Ensemble at the opening of the exhibition (of the same name) of art by the poet. At Canberra Contemporary Artspace, Manuka on 31 August 2017 (Canberra).

'War Cry' (17) - published in the first issue of *Not Very Quiet* online journal of women's poetry and performed at the issue launch on 25 September 2017 at Smith's Alternative (Canberra)

'Cavorting with time' spoken word set - Poems: 1, 4, 8, 17, 18. First performed for the Nimbin Performance Poetry Word Cup heats and grand final on 2 and 3 September 2017 (Nimbin).Performed again for Word in Hand on 7 November 2017 at the Friend in Hand Hotel (Sydney).

'Cavorting with Time' - performance for spoken word and cello, first performed on 30 and 31 March 2018 at the National Folk Festival 2018. Poems: 1, 2, 4, 9, 3, 8, 11, 17, 5, 18. (Canberra).

BIOGRAPHY

Jacqui Malins is a performance poet and artist based in Canberra. Poetry seized her when she saw Candy Royalle perform at the National Folk Festival in 2014. Jacqui went on to be the ACT Poetry Slam winner and an Australian Poetry Slam finalist in 2015, best walk-up poet at the Woodford Festival 2015-16 and a finalist in the Nimbin Performance Poetry World Cup 2017. She has featured at poetry events in Canberra, Sydney and Newcastle. Jacqui is also the co-founder and organiser of Mother Tongue Multilingual Poetry events in Canberra.

My thanks to:

Julia Horvath, whose musicality, creativity and dedication have propelled 'Cavorting with Time' into another dimension.

Shane Strange, of Recent Work Press, who made the idea of a book seem a possible thing.

Caren Florance (Ampersand Duck), whose encouragement, skill and artistry made this book an actual thing.